HENRI WIENIAWSKI

CONCERTO IN D MINOR
OP. 22

PABLO DE SARASATE

ZIGEUNERWEISEN, OP. 20
("GYPSY AIRS")

CONTENTS

To access audio visit:
www.halleonard.com/mylibrary

Enter Code
4552-4717-1178-1442

ISBN 978-1-59615-142-0

Music Minus One

EXCLUSIVELY DISTRIBUTED BY
Hal•Leonard®
7777 W. BLUEMOUND RD. P.O. BOX 13819 MILWAUKEE, WI 53213

© 2005 MMO Music Group, Inc.
All Rights Reserved

For all works contained herein:
Unauthorized copying, arranging, adapting, recording, Internet posting, public performance,
or other distribution of the printed or recorded music in this publication is an infringement of copyright.
Infringers are liable under the law.

Visit Hal Leonard Online at
www.halleonard.com

Henri Wieniawski
Concerto in D minor, Op. 22

HENRI WIENIAWSKI, OPUS 22

DO NOT RUSH

L'Istesso Tempo

CLARINET SOLO AT END OF 22 MEASURES.
DO NOT RUSH

Romance

Violin enters on orchestral
downbeat after clarinet solo.

Andante ma non troppo

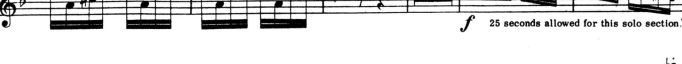

25 seconds allowed for this solo section.

8

Allegro moderato (All zingara)

(start slower)

sul G

tap

ff brillante con fuoco

Pablo De Sarasate
Zigeunerweisen, Op. 20
"Gypsy Airs"

DE SARASATE OPUS 20

The Gypsy style of this piece requires many holds and tempo changes. We advise listening to the complete track, many times, before trying to play along with the audio.

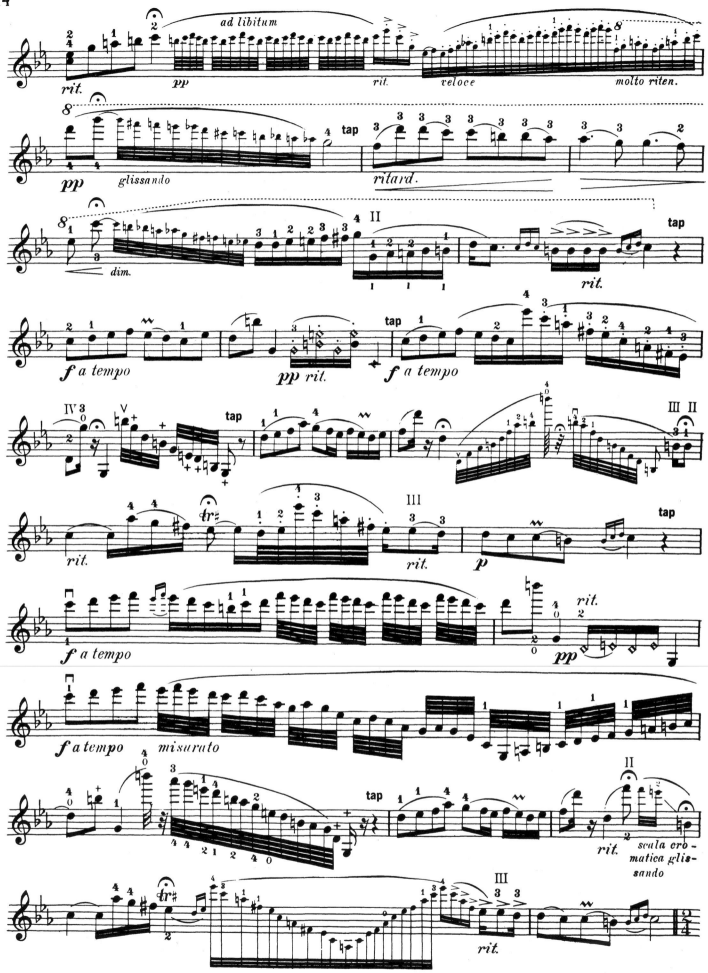

(poco rit.)